ENVIRONMENT

THE ALTRUISTIC MOTHER OF ALL

DR KRISHNAPRADA DASH

This book is dedicated to

DRIEMS Group of Institutions, Tangi, Cuttack, Odisha.

Contents

Preface

Environment: The Altruistic Mother of All is an endeavour to showcase various environmental issues. In this book, the contributors with their thorough research have offered vital contents related to environment. It is a compilation of articles from eminent writers belonging to different fields and students with enormous interest towards academic research. DRIEMS Group of Institutions has taken an initiative to raise an environmental concern amongst the readers.

Acknowledgements

At the outset, I would like to express my deepest gratitude to Dr. Pramod Chandra Rath, the Chairperson of DRIEMS Group of Institutions, for his forever support and guidance to bring this book to the forefront of the readers' community.

My duty lies in expressing earnest salutation to Er. Durga Prasad Rath, the Chairperson, Padmini Care Hospital for his cooperation and motivation in the creation of this book.

I must also exrpess my token of gratefulness to Sj. Balaram Kar, the Director (Admin) of DRIEMS Group of Institutions, for his encouragement to publish this book.

This book *Environment: The Altruistic Mother of All* is an outcome of continuous efforts and inspiration from Er. Sudhansu Bhusan Kar and Prof. Sushanta Kumar Sethy.

- Dr. Krishnaprada Dash

Important Factors influencing the Distribution of Medicinal Flora around Cuttack City

Dr. Kambaska Kumar Behera
Project Director
Gram Samridhi, Kendujhar, Odisha

Cuttack, the oldest city in Odisha, is located at 20°5' N and 85°83' E, close to the east coast of India. The city spread over 398 square kilometers has an average elevation of 36 meters. The city is located at the mouth of the Mahanadi river delta and is surrounded by the Mahanadi River and its tributary Kathjori River. Because of its proximity to the coast, Cuttack has a tropical climate. The temperatures touch 40°C in summer and fall to 10°C in winter. Cyclones and thunder showers are common in monsoon months of July and August. Prior to 1950 the present day Cuttack was prime city of Odia people and its periphery was under a rich forest cover. At present this area is covered with massive office buildings, institutions and residential colonies. The relics of latest erstwhile forest is found at a distance of 20 Kms. During the construction of new institutions the trees along with their stumps were removed the shrubs and annual weeds were cleared. During the last 50 year their has been a great change in the distribution of many flora including some medicinal plants. The objective of present study is to see the distribution of 10 medicinal species in a radius of 20 Kms. Further the studies aim to know the causes of such variability in the distribution pattern, environmental impact relating to automobiles, sewage system and fixing of lights and vegetative and reproductive performance of the species. A brief description of the species are given below.

Strychnos noxvomica L.f., (F-Loganiaceae):A medium to large deciduous trees, the bark, leaf and seeds of which are used in cholera, treatments of wounds and paralytic complaints. The seeds are useful as an appetizer, antiperiodic, digestive, purgative and stomachae. These are also useful in asthma, bronchitis, diabetes, malarial fever, skin diseases and weakness of limbs.

Strychnos potatorum L., (F-Loganiaceae): The clearing nut is a medium size deciduous tree. The seed of which are used in Ayurvedic medicine as an astringent, refrigerant, demulcent, emetic and digestive. There are also useful in nephropathy, apatopathy, renal disorders, diabetes. The powdered bark is used in cholera, and root powdered is used in leprosy.

Alangium salvifolium (L .f) Wang., (F-Alangiaceae): It is a small deciduous small tree or a large shrub. The roots and plants are used in Ayurvedic medicine. The roots are anti-helmintic, thermogenic, diuretic and purgative and antidote for several poison. It is also help full in acute rheumatism and leprosy fruits are purgative and used in burning sensation and hemorrhages.

Premna Obtusifolia R.Br., (F-Verbenaceae): It is a small or deciduous trees. The roots and leaves are used in ayurvedic medicine as a cardiotonic, expectorant, digestive, carminative, antibacterial and tonic besides they are also useful in leprosy and skin diseases flatulens, colic, anorexia diabetes, constipation, It also reduce the blood urea.

Toddalia Asiatica L. Lam ., (F-Rutaceae): It is a prickle rambler herb. The roots, leaves, flowers and fruits are used in various ayurvedic medicine. The roots were digestive, carminative, expectorant, antibacterial and effective in paralysis malarial fever cough, bronchitis, filth ulcer and epilepsy. The unripe fruits were used in vitiated conditions of rheumatism.

Andrographis Paniculata (Burm) Wall.ex.Ness, (F-Acanthaceae): It is an erect annual herb. The whole plant parts used in treating dysentery, diarrhea, fever, sore throat, tonsillitis, bronchitis and hypertension etc.

Cassi occidentialisL., (F-Caesalpiniacea): It is a diffuse offensively odorous shrub. All parts of which used as purgative, expectorant and febrifuge. It is very useful in constipation epilepsy. Roots are digestive and used in stomachae. It is also useful in diabetes, ring worm, leprosy and asthma.

Sida cordifolia L., (F-Malvaceae): It is a much branched under shrub with whitish yellow flowers. The whole plants were used as tonic, and aphrodisiac. It is used in fever fits, colic and nervous disorder. The roots are having healing properties of wounds and also useful in ophthalmic, rheumatism and improve sexual strength.

Evolvulus alsinoides L., (F-Convolvulaceae): It is a perennial herb with prostrate branches. The whole plant contains an alkaloid called shank push pine and one volatile oil. This is useful in general weakness, debility, loss of memory and as a rasayana.

Ocimum basilicum L., (F-Lamiaceae): It is an erect glabrous herb. The leaves and seeds are used in different ayurvedic preparation. The oil extracted from the leaves were used in confectionary bakery goods, tomato ketchup, vinegars, mitts as an beverages. It also used as a flavoring agent in different food preparation.

MATERIAL & METHODS

Selection of plants to study the impact of urbanization was made on the basis of their utility. Plants from different categories like trees, shrubs, annuals etc. were used in the study and described above. The study was confined to North western side of Cuttack city. The impact of urbanization was studied basing on the normal behavior of plants as visualized 50 years back at a distance of 20 Kms.

Basing on their distribution the study was made at a distance of every 4 Kms. Factors responsible for variable distribution of medicinal flora were grouped under clearly visible (10) Sporadic (8) Sparse (6) Rare (4) Not found (2). The cause of such distribution was categorized under self seeding (10), good regeneration (8) poor regeneration (6) Removal for economic value (4) Complete removed (2) Adjustment to the new environment was categorized well adjusted (10) moderate adjusted (6) adjusted (8) poor adjusted (4) Very poor adjust (2). The vegetative and reproductive performance were studied on the basis of very good (6) moderate (4) Poor (2). During the course of investigation all cares were taken to maintain the uniformity for collection of data (Bretschneider, 1898 ; Arnold and De Wet, 1993).

RESULTS AND DISCUSSION

During the course of investigation of the study, it was reveled that *Sida cordifolia* was list affected due to urbanization in the entire length of 20 Kms. The distribution varied from 8.6 to 10. *Strychnos nox-vomica*was almost removed within 4 Kms but fairly maintained up to 20 Kms with increase in distance the plant population increases and its diversity of distribution is of 77±7.0 within 20Kms of radius. However people remove the stumps for using as fuel wood. As regard to the distribution of *Strychnos* *potatorum*, the clearing nut the distribution is poor to very poor i.e.17.4 ± 4.8 within 20Kms of radius because of poor regeneration capacity of seed and whenever a plant was noticed, its vegetative and reproductive performance is very poor. *Strychnos nox-vomica* is more stable then *Strychnos potatorum*. A peculiar investigation was made as regarded to *Alangium salavifolium* that the distribution was better between 8 to 16 Kms. range. It appears that the distribution is associated with habitation and the species is possibly not a forest species, however it sustain the environmental stress and perform moderately for vegetative and reproductive development but the self seedling capacity is responsible for well distribution and diversity of the species is of 71±12.37 within 20Kms. radius. *Toddalia asiatica* were completely vanished within 8Km range and after wards it slowly increase up to 20Km with its distribution index, 22 ± 3.3. The regeneration capacity is poor in the urbanized area and the plants were removed indiscriminately because of thorny appendages in all parts of the plant. It suffered highly due to environmental impact and perform poor for the vegetative and reproductive development. *Andrographis paniculata* normally remove for commercial purpose at present it is only found in the forest or partially denudated forest and poorly or completely distributed to wards the closeness of the city. The distributional index value is of 24.5±5.3 within 20 Kms. radius clearly indicated that the species is also affected by the environmental stress and its vegetative and reproductive performance is also medium to poor. *Evolvulus alsinoides* is almost vanishing at different degree within this 10 Kms of study area although it was not very much affected by environmental stress. But its vegetative and reproductive performance were poor due to constant removal as an annual weed. It is also observed that the weed selects a typical upland situation with good soil or accumulation of natural organics for which it distribution is diminishing and the distributional index value i.e. only 21.8±3.9 within 20 Kms radius of the city. *Ocimum basilicum* was slowly removed with the increase in urbanization and well distributed towards the forest side and its distributional index value is 41.8±4.7. Although its regeneration is very good but its vegetative and reproductive performance is highly affected due to constant removal. However the plant survive to a great degree by sustaining the environmental stress. *Premna obtusifolia* naturally thinly distributed which clearly marked from it distributional value and grown allowing with forest trees. There fore its distribution pattern is poor in the urban area, however the vegetative and reproductive development was moderate. *Cassia occidentalis* the offensive weed slowly vanished in the urban area but the species population increase towards the distal end. However the distributions as well as the vegetative and reproductive development were moderate and the plant sustain effectively to the environmental stress which clearly marked from the distributional index value. The above study concludes that urbanization has definite impact on tree species due to their constant removal and most of the shrubs types were not found because their less ornamental and when ever found all along the fence. The annual medicinal plants are all most moderately distributed except *Sida cordifolia* it prefers to grown on the heart of the city up to 20Km and its distributional index value is 123.9±4.5 and presently this species is also highly affected by various environmental stress including parallel effect of urbanization. Ecological balance in maintaining all the species is feasible by creating one to 2 acres of herbal garden in upland, this will be helpful for providing these valuable noble medicinal flora of the city as well as conservation of the plant for the need of the hour.

CHAPTER TWO

Deforestation and its Extreme Effect on Global Warming

Rosalin Panda
Assistant Project Director
Zilla Parishad, Puri

What is deforestation?

The definition is in the word itself. The prefix de- means "remove", forest is land covered with trees and the suffix-ation means the act or state of. Therefore, deforestation means the act or state of clearing the forest.

What causes deforestation?

There are many reasons people practice deforestation. It could be to give way for agriculture and livestock. It could be for acquiring additional space for housing purposes. It could also be to produce more products like coal, timber, and paper. Whatever the reason is, it only boils down to one culprit – to satisfy human needs.

Did you know?

Did you know that tropical rainforest deforestation adds more carbon dioxide in the atmosphere than cars and trucks? According to the World Carfree Network (WCN), vehicles like cars and trucks account for about 14% of the world's global carbon emissions, while 15% of it, analysts says, are from deforestation alone.

The Food and Agriculture Organization (FAO) reported that an estimate of 53,000 square miles of tropical forests was destroyed every year during the 1980s. Based on this, they estimate that 21,000 square miles were deforested each year in South America and most of this is in the Amazon

Basin. If we are going to use these estimates, the tropical forest will be as cleared annually and it would be as vast as North Carolina!

In addition, a leading green group named the Environmental Defense Fund said that 32 million acres of tropical rainforest were cut down every year between 2000 and 2009 and the numbers are increasing. According to them, if this continues, forest clearing will put another 200 billion tons of carbon into the atmosphere in the coming decades.

What are its effects on global warming?

Many things can happen if we will not prevent or reduce deforestation. First, deforestation affects the amount of oxygen in the atmosphere. Sunlight is essential for photosynthesis, a process where plants absorb sunlight to synthesize food from carbon dioxide and water. Forests help regulate the natural greenhouse effect because trees absorb carbon dioxide from the atmosphere for photosynthesis.

Forests also absorb sunlight and only about 12-15% is reflected whereas deforested areas reflect sunlight by 20%.

Also, the rainforest is very wet and humid. Deforestation will increase the risk of desertification in the cleared areas because trees cover the moist forest soils which prevent it from quickly drying out.

Trees are also responsible for continuing the water cycle by returning water vapour back into the atmosphere.

In addition, some trees are removed by fire. This will add to the amount of carbon dioxide present in the atmosphere.

In conclusion, deforestation affects climate change and global warming because fewer forests mean more carbon dioxide will enter the atmosphere. This will contribute to the increased speed and severity of global warming. The disruption caused by deforestation will lead to more extreme temperature changes that can be harmful to both humans and animals, not to mention that deforestation also ruins the natural habitat of millions of species.

What can we do?

Banning tree-cutting activities are not enough to decrease deforestation. Even if the government will approve laws that would reprimand offenders, people will still take the risk due to economic sense.

People, especially in the third world countries, will not care too much if we are going to convince them to stop logging by presenting its effects. We have to give them an alternative that will stop or decrease logging and, at the same time, helping them improve their livelihood.

United Nations' Reducing Emissions from Deforestation and Forest Degradation or the REDD program aims to establish incentives for the people who will care and protect the forest in order to manage it sustainably while benefitting from it economically.

An example would be introducing alternative livelihood programmes that would require less land (e.g. growing coffees) which will lessen the need for cutting trees.

The participating nations in the REDD programme can accrue and sell carbon pollution credits once they present a proof that deforestation has lowered below the baseline.

Since its inception in 2008, the REDD programme has managed over $117 million in direct financial aid and educational support into national deforestation reduction efforts in 44 developing countries across Africa, Asia, and Latin America.

Brazil, among other participating nations, has shown the significant effect of this project. Through the programme, Brazil was able to slow down deforestation within its borders by 40% and if the momentum continues, the country can increase carbon reduction by 80% in 2020.

If all nations will adapt the REDD programme, reduction of deforestation is possible. This is one way for us to slow down global warming. Again, the solution is in our hands. If people are educated about the effects of deforestation and are given another opportunity to earn a living, the people itself will stop logging. This is indeed a serious matter that every government should give attention to.

CHAPTER THREE

Socio-Economic and Environmental Impacts of Mass Rapid Transit

Prasant Kumar Satapathy
General Manager
FCI, ZO (E), Kolkata

Introduction

The need of Metro system in a city is generally considered necessary when the population of the city exceeds one million. Delhi crossed this milestone in early 1990's and by early 1950's; it was observed that the city's population was doubled which drastically increased the vehicular traffic. By 1990's, Delhi has registered more number of vehicles than Mumbai, Chennai and Kolkata put together. These increased automobiles contributed to more than two third of the city's atmospheric pollution, Delhi turned to become one of the most polluted cities in the World. Due to the above mentioned there aroused an urgent need to analyse and improve the quality and availability of mass transport services.

There are numerous benefits of metro. Some of them are: Time saving for commuters, reliable and safe journey, and reduction in atmospheric pollution, accidents, fuel consumption, vehicle operating cost and also increase in the average speed of road vehicles. The other benefit of the metro is reduced congestion, due to users' shifting from road-based motorized modes to metro systems. This kind of shift naturally results in reduced air pollution and road accidents as well. However, the experience of metro rails in low and middle income counties around the World shows a different scenario. Due to the induced demand, the available road space fills up with motorized vehicles, and the modal shift to metro does not result in the reduction of congestion or air pollution. A study done by the Centre for Science and Environment (CSE) on pollution levels in Delhi illustrate that in 2001 (Delhi Metro started in 2002) the annual average level RSPM, in residential areas was 149 microgram per cubic metre. After registering a drop in 2005, the level rose to 209 microgram per cubic metre in 2008. The concentration is approximately three times higher than safe levels. Similarly, the eight-hourly maximum current level of carbon monoxide (CO) is touching 6,000 microgram per cubic metre, it is way above the safe level of 2,000 microgram per cubic metre, though the annual levels have registered a drop. Overall, these figures illustrate that the operation of the Delhi Metro has not led to a reduction in pollution levels in the city. It is been observed that much of this pollution is caused due to the electricity that is being used by Delhi-metro. It has electricity consumption from traction, running of trains and for non-traction purposes such as lifts, airconditioning of underground stations, lighting of stations, etc. According to 2007 estimate, electricity generation in India contributes 37.8% of CO_2 emissions. Air pollution effects human health adversely and research gives considerable scientific evidence. In a review of epidemiological research that shows how air pollution can lead to damage of central nervous system and may result in decreased cognitive function, low test scores in children, increased risk of autism and neurodegenerative diseases such as Parkinson's and Alzheimer's. Air pollution also leads to cardiovascular disease, and worsens asthma. According to a recent the effect of ambient air quality on children's respiratory system in urban India and found that a rise in particulate matter significantly increases the risk of respiratory ailments. The primary pollutants are CO, NO_2 and RSPM. Hence the present study focuses on the impact of these parameters on the environment.

With the alignment of the Delhi Metro being guided by locations that can be most profitably developed for high-end business parks, the DMRC has become a major property developer with plans to develop the plots of land it has acquired along the route. This is further confirmed by reviewing the funding pattern of the Delhi Metro project (3–7%) from property development) as well as the revenue streams, according to which revenue from real estate contributed as much as half of the total operating revenue during its initial years of operation. The arrival of metros at different locations in Delhi has led to an increase in the real estate prices of areas adjacent to the metro line. According to studies done in 2007–2008, for residential and commercial areas, on average, land value within 500 m of a metro line increased by 11.3% and 18.1%, respectively. Moreover, land value changes are more consistent and higher after a metro is operational, when compared to construction and planning stage, and increase by 2–4% every year.

Materials and Methods

For geo-referencing a rectified map, first three points on the non rectified map were taken and by going to the rectified map, same points are identified and selected. After selecting three such points, the map is geo-referenced and for check, it is observed whether newly geo-referenced map overlays on the map used for rectification.

Step 1: Digitization

The next step involves digitization of all the metro stations on the map along the metro path. This is done by creating a 'point' feature named metrostations.shp and 'polyline' feature named station path using Arc Toolbox and adding the feature in Arc View. Digitizing of all stations and path is performed by selecting option 'Start Editing' in the toolbar. Once all the stations have been digitized, the editing is saved and stopped.

Step 2: Entering the values in Attribute Table

Two attribute tables are created for pre-metro and post-metro. The attribute tables has been prepared in the excel sheet. Post metro excel sheet contains 4 columns namely decrease in NO2, decrease in CO, decrease in RSPM (µg/m3), and increase in land price. Similarly the pre-metro consists of NO2 level, CO level, RSPM (µg/m3) and land price. The excel sheet has been imported in to the attribute table of the shape files by selecting the 'properties' of the shape file and using the command 'join' and 'relates', followed by the command 'join the table' where the excel sheet is selected and joined. The same procedure is followed for both the excel sheets.

Step 3: Symbology

In this step, the parameters are displayed. By selecting the layer properties→ display → select field, desired field that should be shown on the map is selected. To display the field in terms of desired symbols, shapes, and classes; go to layer properties→ symbology→ quantities→ graduated symbols; here one can select the required number of classes and symbols.

Step 4: Interpolation

The interpolation commands are as follows:

Select geo-processing→ geo statistical analysis→ interpolation→ IDW select the required field i.e. NO2 levels, CO levels, land price and RSPM.

As mentioned above, the features given in symbology are used for representation and classification of fields. Transparency option is used to clearly show the interpolation and the stations. Transparency of 40-50 % is applied.

Step 5: Clipping

To show the target area and fields more clearly, the area between the two target stations is clipped from the whole map. For this go to Arc Tool box→ extract→ Clip. In the clip give input features, here make a shape file of polygon feature and select the desired area to be clipped and apply. In this way the clipped image has been obtained. Here the clipping is done for Raster layer.

Step 6: Comparison

To enable comparison between pre metro and post metro and for convenience, all the shape files of pre metro and post metro are imported to the menu box, due to which the desired field can be simultaneously shown in pre metro and post metro situation.

Results and Discussions

The present study analyzes the metro rail condition in a city and its effect on environment and socio factors. It is observed several operations of metros like maintenance of infrastructure, and construction of rail tracks significantly impacts the metro rail energy consumption and emissions. These emissions have adverse impact on the environment. It also appears that metro's overall negative impact on the environment is higher than the CNG-run bus systems, Delhi. Although there has been reduction in the values of CO, NO2 and RSPM for the postmetro condition but these values are expected to rise owing to several operations of metros mentioned above. However, there is a significant growth in the Land price at all places in the study area. It is relevant to note that the results emanated from the present paper are based on the chosen input parameters, which may vary for various locations. However, methodology and analysis remains same which is the main focus of the present study, which helps in proposing necessary mitigation strategies.

Conclusions

In the present study, ArC Geographical Information Systems (GIS) software has been used to perform the comparative analysis of Pre- MRTS (Mass Rapid Transit System) and Post-MRTS (Mass Rapid Transit System) with respect to Environmental and Socio-economic factors in a metropolitan city. GIS provides very fast access to very large spatial databases for a large number of users, at the same time maintaining the spatial data using standard DBMS technology. The software also provides a framework for directly map, query, analyze, and edit data maintained in a geo-database.

The study helps the planners to have the complete view of the pre-metro and post-metro status of the environment and thus environment planning and policies formulation can be done in a sustainable way. GIS representation helps in identifying the critical areas which requires immediate attention in terms of improving the quality of environment with respect to the selected parameters. The study serves as a model to analyze the environmental impact of Delhi metro within some given radius around the area where metro is operating. The study also provides as a tool for comparison of impact of metro at different areas in a particular state or a city simultaneously and thus allows different scenarios to be investigated quickly and efficiently.

To establish the model and methodology, study deals with few important environment and socio-economic factors which can be enhanced easily.

CHAPTER FOUR

The Five Elements and Seven Chakras of Human Body and their Positive Effects on the Environments

Shringarmani Rashmi Rekha Dash
Assistant Professor
Sri Sri University

A lot of ancient philosophies around the globe classify the composition of the Universe into 5 elements: Earth, Water, Fire, Air, and Ether (Space). These are also called the "Panch Mahabhoot." Knowledge of these five elements helps us understand the laws of nature.

Each of the five elements represents a state of matter in nature. Solid matter is classified as the "Earth" element. Water is everything that is liquid. Air is everything that is gas. Fire is that part of Nature that transforms one state of matter into another. Ether is the mother of the other elements and is the basis of higher spiritual experiences.

Earth forms solid structures such as teeth, nails, bones, muscles, skin, tissues, and hair. These give structure and strength to the body. Water forms saliva, urine, semen, blood, and sweat. Fire forms hunger, thirst, sleep, the vision in the eyes, and the complexion of the skin. Air is responsible for all movement including expansion, contraction, vibration, and suppression. Space is the subtlest of all elements and is present in the hollow cavities of the body in the form of radio frequencies, light radiation, cosmic rays, etc.

Imbalance of Water element: This is visible as excess mucus, cold, sinusitis, swelling of glands, edema of tissues, blood thinning, or blood clotting.

Imbalance of Earth element: shows itself as general weakness in the body, loss of calcium from bones, obesity, cholesterol, weight loss, weight gain, muscular diseases, etc.

Imbalance of Fire element: manifests itself as fever, skin diseases like inflammation, increased coldness or heat in the body, excessive sweating, hyper-acidity, slow digestion and absorption of nutrients, toxins in the body, diabetes, etc.

Imbalance of Air elements: leads to skin dryness, blood pressure problems, lung disorders, dry cough, bloating, constipation, lethargy, insomnia, muscular spasms, depression, etc.

Imbalance of Space element: is visible as Thyroid disorders, throat problems, speech disorders, epilepsy, madness, ear diseases, etc.

Chakras are energy centers/vortexes in the body that impact the physical, mental, emotional, financial, sexual, behavioral, social, environmental, and spiritual aspects of our well-being.

There are hundreds of chakras in our body but we focus on seven main ones for healing purposes. The energy that keeps us going, flows through these chakras as they store and distribute energy. There are seven main chakras along the spine and each chakra is associated with specific organs, systems, and glands in the body. Every chakra has a specific color and element.

These seven chakras are responsible for creating our lives. When all the main seven chakras are aligned and are working together, there is harmony in our lives at all levels. When our chakras are blocked, imbalanced, or out of alignment, the free energy flow is obstructed which can lead to physical, emotional, mental, or spiritual dis-ease.

Muladhara Chakra is connecting to Earth Element.

Location: Base of the spine between the anus and genitals.

How it affects the body: The Muladhara Chakra influences the health of the bones, teeth, nails, anus, prostate, adrenals, kidneys, lower digestive functions, excretory functions, and sexual activity.

Swadishthana Chakra is connecting to Water Element:

Location: Situated at the base of the pubis between the genitals and the sacral nerve plexus

How it affects the body: The Swadishthana Chakra deals with the individual's emotional identity, creativity, desire, pleasure and self-gratification, procreation, and personal relationships.

It governs the sexual organs, stomach, upper intestines, liver, gallbladder, kidney, pancreas, adrenal glands, spleen, middle spine, and autoimmune system.

An unbalanced Swadishthana Chakra leads to lower back pain, sciatica, decreased libido, pelvic pain, urinary problems, poor digestion, low resistance to infection and viruses, tiredness, hormonal imbalances, and menstrual problems.

Manipura Chakra is connecting to Fir Element:

Location: At the level of the umbilicus corresponding to the gastric or solar plexus

How it affects the body: Manipura Chakra deals with a sense of belonging, and mental understanding of emotions, and defines self-esteem in an individual.

It governs the effective functioning of the upper abdomen, gallbladder, liver, middle spine, kidney, adrenals, small intestines, and stomach.

An unbalanced Manipura Chakra may lead to diabetes, pancreatitis, adrenal imbalances, arthritis, colon diseases, stomach ulcers, intestinal tumors, anorexia/bulimia, or low blood pressure.

Anahata Chakra is connecting to Air Element:

Location: On the cardiac plexus in the region of the heart

How it affects the body: Anahata Chakra affects a person's social identity and influences traits like trust, forgiveness, unconditional love, wisdom, compassion, and issues of the soul.

It deals with the functioning of the heart, rib cage, blood, circulatory system, lungs and diaphragm, thymus gland, breasts, esophagus, shoulders, arms, and hands.

An imbalance can cause issues related to the thoracic spine, upper back and shoulder problems, asthma, heart conditions, shallow breathing, and lung diseases.

Vishuddhi Chakra is connecting to Ether Element:

Location: On the level of the throat, the nerve plexus of the pharynx region

How it affects the body: Vishuddhi Chakra deals with personality traits like communication, creativity, faith, truthfulness, self-awareness, and expression.

It governs the throat, the thyroid, parathyroid gland, trachea, cervical vertebrae, vocal cords, neck and shoulders, arms, hands, esophagus, mouth, teeth, and gums.

An unbalanced Vishuddhi Chakra causes thyroid dysfunctions, sore throat, stiff neck, mouth ulcers, gum or tooth problems, laryngitis, and hearing problems.

Ajna Chakra is connecting to Light Element:

Location: Between the eyebrows (third eye)

How it affects the body: Ajna Chakra deals with self-awareness, wisdom, intellect, clairvoyance, implementation of ideas, detachment, insight, understanding, and intuitive reasoning.

It governs the functions of the brain, eyes, ears, nose, pituitary gland, pineal glands, and the neurological system. Any imbalance could lead to headaches, nightmares, eyestrain, learning disabilities, panic, depression, blindness, deafness, seizures, or spinal dysfunctions.

Sahasrara Chakra is connected to the conscience Element:

Sahasrara Chakra influences intuitive knowledge, connection to spirituality, integration of mind-body-spirit, and conscious awareness.

It governs the center of the head and midline above the ears, brain, nervous system, and pineal gland.

Chakras are associated with the organs and glands of the particular region where they are located. As such, they have a strong bearing on our health, our mental state, and our relation with others. Based on various factors such as our lifestyle, environment and surroundings, past experiences, etc., the chakras can either be balanced or imbalanced. If a chakra is imbalanced, it goes into either a hypoactive or a hyperactive mode. A hypoactive or blocked chakra's functioning is either insufficient or reduced. Likewise, a hyperactive chakra means there is too much energy flowing into that particular region, and as such, there is an imbalance in the overall flow of energy throughout the body.

Since chakras are interrelated, when one of them is imbalanced, it causes a disturbance in the functionality of the other chakras as well. This makes people feel disconnected, anxious, and fearful, and it also manifests as health problems in one or more areas of the body.

To function at their best, your chakras need to be balanced. And for this, you need to know what the chakras actually do and what are some of the things you can do to take care of them.

The chakras act as distribution centers. They distribute the five pranas to their associated local regions. For example, the root chakra will distribute the 'Apana prana' to the pelvic region and provide energy for the organs in this region. When a chakra is blocked or not functioning properly, this distribution pattern gets disturbed, and physical or psycho-emotional/energy issues arise.

Imbalance is a part of life, however, regular practice of yoga asanas will help you balance your chakras, enabling you to live a fulfilled, contented, and happy life in the pink of health!

CHAPTER FIVE

Orphan

Saroj Kumar Sahoo
Arieotech Solutions

Orphan Environment!

All are worried to save environment, plant trees and save jungle, hill and soil. This is only limited in pen, paper and in our mind. We have time to destroy the jungle, We have time to destroy plants, We have time to cut the branch, stem of tree, but We don't have time to plant a single tree.

I have time to plant only in front of media, camera and more over to take selfie to impress my friends and relatives. This is not our fault to care the plant, care the environment or care the society.

Our education system only teaches how to get job, get good status and increase your social reputation through money. These types of mentality has been implemented from our child hood.
How can we prevent us from all these thought and actions?

But I am optimistic on our coming generation and beautiful flowers which are ready to understand the moral of environment, plants, pure air, oxygen, hill and soil. They understand, feel the lack of nature's nurture in form of polluted air, dirty water, sand sliding and many more problem which are facing in day to day life like lungs issue, cough, breath problem etc.

We already lost jewel which is more powerful, more expensive than the Kohinoor and our life line to live or save life that's only our ENVIRONMENT. We can't leave it as orphan. And, our collective responsibility
to save our life by saving our environment, jungle, water, soil and air.

Lets promise and take the challenge to create more robust energies society to trained them, education them to save our JEWEL which is our ENVIRONMENT.

CHAPTER SIX

Frontriers of Environmental Study

Pooja Mohapatra
Lecturer, Department of Biology
DRIEMS

The increasing urbanization and alienation from nature reduce children's opportunities to interact with plants and challenge teachers to devise educational practice that contribute to learning botany. The methods of teaching botany in context and link student's specific knowledge to values and practices that contribute to an environmental education that aims to minimize the utilitarian view of nature and move towards a view of human beings as non-living elements.

The Earth does not belong to us. We belong to the earth - Marlee Matlin.

Frontiers of environmental science emphasis on research at the cutting edge of knowledge of our natural world and its various interaction with society. It is the bridge between the identification and measurement of change, comprehension of the processes responsible and measures needed to reduce their impact. It is aim is to assist the formulation of policies by offering sound scientific evidence on environmental science that will lead to a more inhabitable and sustainable world for the generations of education to come. The natural resources are the practical teachers of the environment studies.

CHAPTER SEVEN

Coastal Flooding by "2100"

Rudraprasad Sahoo
Lecturer, Department of Zoology
DRIEMS

The climate crisis is warming the Arctic more than twice as fast as any where else on the planet. Today sea levels are rising more than twice as quickly as they did for most of the 20th century as a result of increasing temperature on Earth Seas are now rising of 32 mm per year globally and they will continue to grow upto about of 0.7 meters by the end by of this century. In the Arctic, the green Land ice shut poses the greater risk for sea levels because hitting land ice is the main cause of rising sea levels.

According to satellite data, the Greenland ice sheet lost a record amount of ice in 2019, an average of a million tons per minute throughout the years. One of the biggest environmental problem that cascading effect. If the entire Greenland ice sheet melts sea level would rise by 6 meters.

The sea level rise will have a divesting impact, on those living in coastal region According to research sea level rise this century could flood coastal areas that are now home to 340 million to 480 million people, forcing them to migrate to safer areas and contributing to overpopulation and strain of resources in the areas they migrate to.

Take Shanghai, China's for Examples, which is built around the Low-Lying Yangtze river delta. As the fourth most populous city in the world, the flood risk in the area is high due to its geographical position. Any flooding caused by higher rainfall can potentially be catastrophic in relation to evacuation, water management & property damage.

"One of the first condition of happiness is that the link between man & nature shall not be broken."

CHAPTER EIGHT

The Role of Environmental Engineers in the Fight Against Air Pollution

Jagadish Sutar
7th **Semester, Electrical Engineering**
DRIEMS

Pollution, also called environmental pollution, the addition of any substance (solid, liquid, or gas) or any form of energy (such as heat, sound, or radioactivity) to the environment at a rate faster than it can be dispersed, diluted, decomposed, recycled, or stored in some harmless form. The major kinds of pollution, usually classified by environment, are air pollution, water pollution, and land pollution. Modern society is also concerned about specific types of pollutants, such as noise pollution, light pollution, and plastic pollution. Pollution of all kinds can have negative effects on the environment and wildlife and often impacts human health and well-being.

Air pollution is increasing at a rapid rate across the world, wreaking havoc with the environment and the health of humans. In fact, every year an estimated 4.2 million people die globally every year as a result of exposure to outdoor air pollution, according to the World Health Organization (WHO). The rapid increase in pollution can, in part, be attributed to the swift economic development enjoyed in many areas across the globe. At present, nearly 80% of the world's urban population is believed to live in cities that have unacceptable levels of air pollution. While there are many contributors to the poor air quality, engineering and manufacturing concerns are at the top of the list. Thankfully, there are a group of professionals within the engineering sector, known as environmental engineers, who not only identify pollutants but design systems to contain them as well.

Careful analysis leads to greater understanding:

When a new manufacturing concern is being built, a team of environmental engineers will be tasked with identifying the various compounds utilized in the production process. The pollutants that will be generated will also be determined. While such an in-depth analysis may seem inconsequential, it is a vital step towards the containment of pollutants. After the analysis has been concluded, a range of statistical models can be created that link fuels and contaminants to levels of air pollution.

Find solutions to key issues:

The role of an environmental engineer is not only to identify common air pollutants, but also to design and enforce effectual solutions. There are a number of control mechanisms that can be utilized to reduce the amount of pollutants emitted by a manufacturing plant. Recommending the installation of air pollution equipment such as thermal oxidizers can prove to be very beneficial. These oxidizers are capable of destroying high-volume Volatile Organic Compounds (VOCs) and Hazardous Air Pollutants (HAPs) that are created during a variety of industrial exhaust streams and chemical processes. Other measures to consider include complex ventilation systems and baghouses that can be used at steel mills and pharmaceutical companies.

Global engineering efforts for a cleaner future:

Engineers from across the globe are focusing their efforts on developing technologies that can reduce air pollution and improve human and environmental health. Engineers in Israel developed a pioneering application entitled BreezoMeter which has now gained popularity all across the world. The app offers personalized air quality as well as pollen-related data and fire alerts. Coverage is worldwide and data is accurate all the way down to street level. BreezoMeter utilizes the power of big data and can pinpoint sources of extensive air pollution. Over in Beijing, China, projects such as the Smog-Free Tower is aiming to decrease air pollution in the country which sees more than 1.6 million people dying every year due to pollution-related illnesses. The tower sucks 30,000 m3/hr of air pollution and compresses the residue which is then, somewhat surprisingly, molded into jewelry items such as rings and cufflinks.

People die annually from pollution:

Air pollution is estimated to kill 7 million people every year. Radioactive and toxic waste in water can cause many diseases, including fatal conditions such as typhoid fever and cholera. Consumption of contaminated water causes approximately 485,000 deaths every year. In conclusion, there are many ways to reduce pollution on earth namely practicing the 3Rs concept, reduce the usage of vehicles on road, creating awareness among citizens, and enforcing the laws which will create a better environment for the benefits of both mankind and our mother earth.

CHAPTER NINE

Berlin's Urban Evolution

Abhishek Nanda
2nd Semester, Computer Science Engineering
DRIEMS

Germany's largest city has reinvented itself many times in its 785-year history. Now, it must do so once again in the face of climate change.

For three weeks last summer, Berliners coming to exercise at Wilmersdorf Stadium were greeted by a strangely bucolic scene. Sheep were grazing where the former grandstands had once stood, feeding where soccer fans had once cheered — their gentle bleating a surprising and pastoral note in the busy urban soundscape.

The animals were part of a pilot project initiated by the Charlottenburg-Wilmersdorf District's Department of Nature Conservation and The Nature Conservancy's Urban Greening Program, which launched in Germany in 2020 with a roughly $4 million gift from Amazon. Wilmersdorf Stadium offered a chance to enhance urban biodiversity while also testing an inexpensive and low-carbon form of landscape maintenance. That maintenance had become necessary after the stadium, built as a community athletic facility in the mid 20th century to host 50,000 spectators — a capacity it never reached — removed its grandstands in the 1990s. Over time the newly exposed ground on the stadium's embankments became overgrown with invasive box elder and other difficult-tocontrol species. In response, local conservation officials suggested the parks authority try sheep. The animals would both manage the invasives and leave a more diversified landscape in their wake, helping the hillside eventually evolve into an urban grassland and provide habitat for native insects and other wildlife. For the district, it is a novel approach to repurposing an urban space. But looking to the restorative power of nature is an idea with deep roots in Berlin. Today, green space makes up nearly a third of the German capital. The city's rooftops buzz with urban beehives, and bicycling accounts for more than 13% of all traffic, twice the share of U.S. cycling hotspot Portland, Oregon. As climate change brings new challenges, Berlin is looking to its history as a laboratory for understanding urban nature to chart a path forward.

Since Germany reunified in 1990, Berliners have often made parks and green spaces from the city's former ruins. Part of the oncemilitarized, now-fallow border strip of the former Berlin Wall has been designated as a landscape conservation area and is being transformed into a 9-mile-long chain of parks, meadows and urban woodlands. Meanwhile, the runways and fields of Berlin's century-old Tempelhof Airport, which closed in 2008, have been reborn as a 740-acre public gathering space — areas of which are also grazed by sheep. The instinct to allow nature to reclaim disused spaces in the city stems in part from Berlin's history as a pioneer in establishing the value of biodiversity in cities. "Berlin is called the cradle of urban ecology," says Ulrich Heink, the head of the Charlottenburg Wilmersdorf Department of Nature Conservation. In the 1970s, an ecologist named Herbert Sukopp began studying the vegetation that had sprung up in the "Brachen," or fallow spaces, of Berlin's urban fabric. Over time, Sukopp succeeded in demonstrating that cities, far from being denuded wastelands, are rich in species and often develop novel ecosystems distinct from those outside the city limits. "He introduced the idea of urban ecology worldwide," Heink says. In the coming century, cities like Berlin will only become more important as refuges for vulnerable species. Some species have already carved out ecological niches for themselves. Peregrine falcons, for instance, exhibit higher rates of reproductive success in urban areas than in rural ones. According to an international team of researchers, cities can even foster larger and more diverse bee populations than the surrounding countryside. All of this makes reclaimed natural spaces like those being cultivated at Wilmersdorf Stadium important green pockets throughout the city. "Urban sites have huge potential for nature conservation," Heink says.

The stadium project is one of several investments being made through TNC's Urban Greening Program. According to Jamie Chan, who is leading the program, TNC is also working with local officials in Berlin, Stuttgart and a third, yet-to-be-announced municipality in Germany to identify opportunities for green infrastructure and other nature-based solutions that can help mitigate severe effects of climate change. In Berlin, that means addressing urban flooding, extreme heat, and access to green space, says

Rob McDonald, the lead scientist for nature-based solutions at TNC. Scientists predict that a warmer climate will produce more frequent and severe storms, as Europe saw in 2021, when catastrophic flooding tore through several countries, including Belgium and Germany, killing more than 200 people. Of equal concern, McDonald says, are deadly heat waves — already the most fatal of all weather events. Northern European cities ill-adapted to hot climates will be hit especially hard, says McDonald. "Nobody has air-conditioning, you're in big stone buildings often, and when you get heat events that last multiple days, they become like ovens." Warmer temperatures will affect more than the city's human inhabitants. In the summer, Berlin can be as much as 9 degrees warmer than areas outside the city, creating an environment in which non-native species from hotter climates can thrive. "We can bemoan this situation and call it unnatural," Heink says. "But it's also a chance to have a very specific flora and fauna, which is part of what forms the biological identity of Berlin. There's potential in that." Heink and the scientists at TNC planned for just such a future at Wilmersdorf. In the seed mix used to revegetate the stadium's former grandstand areas were seeds of species native to warmer climates — a hedge against the coming heat. A team from the Technical University of Berlin will monitor the project and measure changes in biodiversity over time. For now, Heink is pleased with one of the unexpected benefits of the sheep: public delight. For the three weeks the animals were present, they served as incidental ambassadors of the kind of work his department and TNC are trying to do. Families with small children seemed to spend as much time watching the sheep as they did playing. "When the sheep were there, everybody was fond of them," Heink says. "I think [the project] has huge potential in terms of environmental education."

A Gentler Lawnmower: In the 1990s officials removed some of the old bleacher seats from Wilmersdorf Stadium, a community athletics facility. On one side of the stadium, a vineyard was planted where the old grandstands had stood. On the other side, grasses grew into a weedy field. In summer 2021, to combat invasive weeds and create a meadow of native plants, the local parks authority brought in a small herd of sheep to graze.

Wildlife in the City: Urban ecology — a field of study that gained early traction in Berlin — has shown that cities can develop ecosystems distinct from more rural areas nearby. In Berlin, hundreds of wild bee species flit among green spaces around the city that are also home to boars, white-tailed eagles, grey herons and red foxes. By some estimates there are more fox dens within the city limits than in nearby forests.

New Normal: In 2021, catastrophic flooding in northern Europe killed more than 200 people, and heat waves threatened multiple countries. In Berlin, inner-city areas can be 9 degrees warmer than surrounding rural areas, making green spaces like parks and streams important refuges. Resident Leon Stiebl (above right) cools down in a fountain at Marheinekeplatz at the peak of a heat wave that hit the city in June 2021. And on one of the hottest days of the year, city residents (above left) listen to a soccer game as they soak in a stream near a Viktoriapark waterfall.

Redefining Space: Berlin's history is visible in its cityscape in ruins and monuments to past events. City residents have chosen to turn some disused areas into communal green space. Along the former Berlin Wall, fallow ground is being converted into a 9-mile chain of parks and meadows. And on the banks of the Spree River (above), biking paths, soccer fields and communal spaces make up the 6-acre Spreebogenpark. Located near German legislative buildings, the park pays homage to an embassy district that Hitler's regime cleared for a planned "world capital." Only the Swiss embassy remains.

The People's Parks: Once key to the Berlin Airlift of 1948 and 1949 that kept the city's west side viable during a Communist blockade, Tempelhof Airport ceased operations in 2008. In response, the citizens of Berlin successfully fought for the runway fields to be turned into a public park. Now the site, known as Tempelhofer Feld, is the largest inner-city open space in the world and is home to community gardens, athletic fields and other public gathering spaces.

Author

Dr. Krishnaprada Dash is currently working as the Head, Department of Humanities & Social Sciences, DRIEMS (Autonomous). She has pioneered two Literary Clubs namely Jigruksha for DRIEMS Management Wing and Tvastra for DRIEMS (Autonomous). She is also the Founder of Adhyashay Literary Club.